SULEYMAN
AND THE
OTTOMAN
EMPIRE

John Addison

Greenhaven World History Progra

GENERAL EDITORS

Malcolm Yapp
Margaret Killingray
Edmund O'Connor

Cover design by John Castle

ISBN 0-89908-013-8 Paper Edition
ISBN 0-89908-038-3 Library Edition

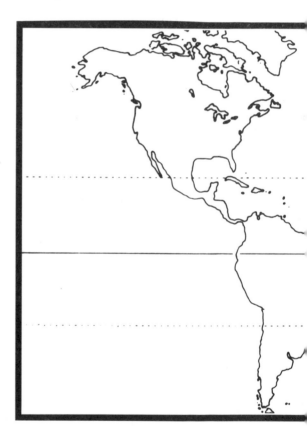

First published in Great Britain 1974 by
GEORGE G. HARRAP & CO. LTD
© George G. Harrap & Co. Ltd 1974

SULEYMAN AND THE OTTOMAN EMPIRE

by John Addison

Greenhaven Press, Inc.
577 SHOREVIEW PARK ROAD
ST. PAUL, MN 55112

Sultan Suleyman the Magnificent

In November 1553, Anthony Jenkinson, an English merchant traveller, happened to be in Aleppo in Syria when the army of the Ottoman Sultan Suleyman passed through the city on its way to fight the Persians. Jenkinson had travelled widely. He knew the great rulers of the time – Henry VIII of England, Francis I of France, Charles V the Holy Roman Emperor and Akbar the Great, the Mughal Emperor in India. None of these rulers and nothing he had seen in their countries had impressed him so much as the sight of Suleyman and his great army. The climax came when the Sultan himself rode by: 'Then came the Great Turke himselfe, with great pompe and magnificence, using in his countenance and gesture a

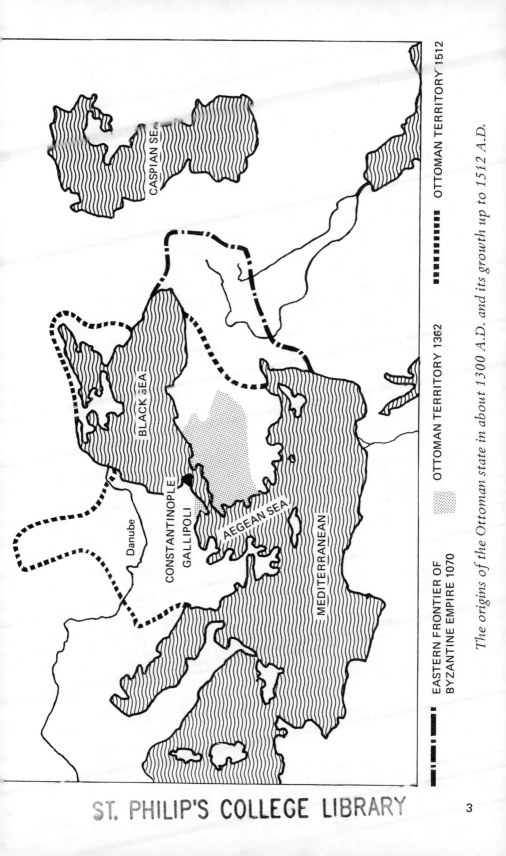

CASPIAN SEA

BLACK SEA

Danube

CONSTANTINOPLE
GALLIPOLI

AEGEAN SEA

MEDITERRANEAN

EASTERN FRONTIER OF
BYZANTINE EMPIRE 1070

OTTOMAN TERRITORY 1362

OTTOMAN TERRITORY 1512

The origins of the Ottoman state in about 1300 A.D. and its growth up to 1512 A.D.

3

wonderfull majestie'. He was watching the greatest ruler of the day. His empire was at the height of its power. Who were the Ottomans? How had they come to rule such an empire?

THE TURKS

The Ottomans were part of the Turkish peoples. Turkish nomads had been moving westwards from the steppelands of central Asia into the Muslim lands of western Asia ever since the eighth century. They became Muslims themselves and came to rule the Muslim lands. As soldiers they took on the task of fighting the Christians. The greatest Christian power in the Middle East was Byzantium. Byzantium was the state which had once formed the Eastern Roman Empire. (On Eastern Roman Empire: *Constantine*)* Its capital was Constantinople where Asia and Europe meet, and its land lay in Asia Minor and southeast Europe. It was against the Byzantine Empire that the Turkish Muslims fought. In the fourteenth century there were a number of small Turkish states in Asia Minor who carried on the war against Byzantium. One of these was ruled by Osman, or Othman Beg. His followers were called Ottomans. It was this little state on the shores of the Aegean Sea that was to grow in two centuries into a great Empire.

THE RISE OF THE OTTOMAN EMPIRE

The Ottoman state had a special place in the Muslim lands. Othman

Beg's followers were the advance guard of the world of Islam against the world of the Christians. They were *ghazis* — warriors — waging almost constant war. To be one of the ghazis brought a man not only prestige but also a chance of plunder. More Muslims placed themselves under Othman and the little state grew. By 1354 the Ottomans had won their first foothold in Europe at Gallipoli. In the early fourteenth century the Ottomans met with a check, but in 1451, when Mehemed II became Sultan, the Ottomans began to prepare a new advance. Mehemed decided that his first duty was to capture Constantinople.

THE OTTOMAN TURKS CAPTURE CONSTANTINOPLE

From the moment that the Ottomans set foot on the northern side of the straits of the Dardanelles Constantinople was doomed. It was gradually surrounded. The Sultan began to mass his armies outside the land walls on the west side of the city. (D1)**

The seige lasted from 6th April to 29th May 1453. At one point Mehemed had seventy ships dragged overland on rollers from the Bosphorus so that he could control the Golden Horn. Towards the end of May the Sultan prepared for the final assault. On 28th May the defenders saw omens of approaching disaster. A terrible storm broke over the city and weird lights played over the church of Santa Sophia. That evening the last Christian service

*Titles in brackets refer to other booklets in the Program
* *The reference (D) indicates the numbered documents at the end of this book

| OTTOMAN SULTANS | | THE NEW CAPITAL, ISTANBUL |

OTTOMAN SULTANS

1281-1324	A.D.	Osman I
1451-1481		Mehmed II The Conqueror
1481-1512		Bayezid II
1512-1520		Selim I The Grim
1520-1566		Suleyman I The Magnificent

THE NEW CAPITAL, ISTANBUL

Constantinople had been in decline for a long time before the seige. Nevertheless, it was still a great city. Nothing could take away its magnificent setting and its position at the meeting place of so many different routes by land and sea. No single event was as important as its capture in the rise of the Ottoman Empire. It had for so long been the capital of the world of the Christian enemy. Now it would become the capital of a Muslim empire.

Its capture brought Mehemed instant glory and prestige. He was Mehemed the Conqueror. Since he had captured the old capital of the Roman Empire would he not now take over all that had once

was held in the great cathedral. Early on 29th May the Turks hoisted the Ottoman flag over the ruined walls and broke into the city.

Constantinople at the time of the siege, 1453

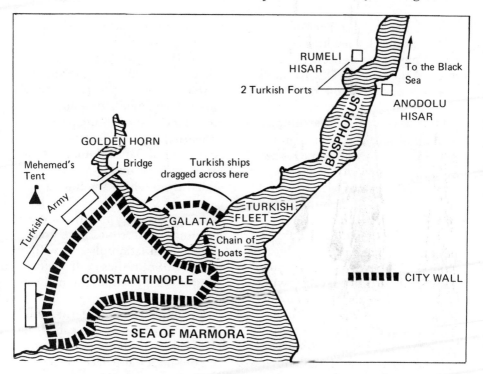

Panoramic view of Istanbul

belonged to Rome? The Sultan had great ambitions; he was beginning to see himself as the ruler of the world. (D2) Istanbul (for this was the name the Muslims gave the city) must be made a capital worthy of a great Empire. Few cities have such a magnificent position. It was built on a wedge of land between two stretches of water – the Sea of Marmora and the Golden Horn. Several hills added to its attractions.

The Sultan tried to attract people to come and live in his new capital: 'Whoever wishes let him come and let him become owner of houses, vineyards and gardens in Istanbul.' Few people came. Then the governors of all the provinces were told to order families to come to Istanbul. New

buildings were started and the city began to grow.

The finest buildings were religious ones and the mosques were the most important of these. One of Mehemed's first actions on entering Constantinople was to convert the great Christian Cathedral of Santa Sophia into a mosque. Four *minarets* were added from which the muezzin called the faithful to prayer. By the reign of Suleyman there were hundreds of mosques both great and small in Istanbul – all with minarets. Soon these tall slender columns had become the main feature of any view of the city.

Mehemed the conqueror built himself a palace. It was called the New Palace to distinguish it from the old imperial palace in the centre of the city. It was also known as the Topkapi Palace; a vast collection of buildings, courtyards and gardens where the Sultan, his family and his large household of officials and guards lived. It remained the centre of the court and government until the nineteenth century.

The climax of the Ottomans' achievement in building as in so much else came in the reign of Suleyman the Magnificent. The greatest of all Ottoman builders was Mimar Sinan. He claimed that he had erected 312 buildings. Most of these were mosques, but they included buildings like schools, colleges, tombs, palaces, bridges, bathhouses and *caravanserai*. The last were like large inns or hostels paid for by the State for the use of travellers. They were common in the Muslim world. Such caravanserai provided shelter for pilgrims going to the Holy Places of Mecca and Medina. *(Muhammad and the Arab Empire)*

Sinan was first of all a soldier, a member of the famous corps of *Janissaries*. He showed his building skill constructing bridges on military campaigns. He was appointed chief architect of Sultan Suleyman, and spent the rest of his his life designing and building for Suleyman and Sultan Selim II. The finest of his buildings was the great mosque named after the sultan the 'Suleymaniye' Mosque. (D3) Its beauty was increased by the use of different coloured stones. Tiles glazed in brilliant colours were used to decorate it. Sometimes these were arranged in geometrical patterns, sometimes they represented flowers, leaves and

The interior of Santa Sophia — the church which became a mosque

plants; and very often they formed Arabic script with texts from the *Koran,* the Muslim holy book. The potters who made the tiles also made beautiful jugs, bowls and plates.

Like all great mosques the Suleymaniye was surrounded by other buildings. These included several schools and students' hostels, a bathhouse and a hospital, almshouses and a caravanserai. A Turkish writer in the seventeenth century took much delight in describing how

7

western visitors marvelled at Sinan's great masterpiece. (D4)

THE EXPANSION OF THE EMPIRE

As Istanbul grew the empire itself expanded. At the beginning of the sixteenth century the Ottomans were faced with serious rivals in the Muslim world. These were the Safavids, the new rulers of Persia. It looked also as though they might be joined by a second enemy of the Ottomans. These were the Mamluk rulers of Egypt and Syria.

In this crisis it was fortunate that the new Ottoman Sultan, Selim I, the father of Suleyman, was a great warrior. He earned the nickname of 'the Grim'. He marched against Persia in 1514, and two years later against the Mamluks. He defeated both. The whole of the Mamluk Empire, including the holy cities of Mecca and Medina, was taken over by the Ottomans. In Selim's short reign the empire doubled in size. The Ottoman Sultan had a stronger claim than ever to be regarded as the head of the world of Islam. All these recent gains, however, had been made at the expense of the other Muslims. It was time that the Ottomans renewed their earlier claims to leadership of Islam. These had depended on their success as ghazis, warriors in the Holy War against the infidel (non-Muslim). Selim had every intention of doing this. He was planning a campaign against the European Christians when he died in 1520.

View of the Topkapi Palace which housed Mehemed and his family

SULEYMAN THE MAGNIFICENT AND HIS WARS

Suleyman came to the throne at a time of great opportunity. He was also lucky. The Christian kings of the West were facing difficulties. Charles V, Holy Roman Emperor, King of Spain, ruler of Burgundy, the Netherlands and of Spain's lands in the Americas, seemed very powerful. But his scattered lands were difficult to protect. A German monk, Martin Luther, had started a movement in the Church, which led to the split between Protestants and Catholics. (On the Reformation: *Luther, Erasmus and Loyola*) Whole areas of Europe followed Luther as Protestants and challenged the power of Catholic kings like Charles. In 1521 Charles quarelled with Francis I of France and they went to war. The two

The Suleymaniye Mosque

greatest monarchs in Christian Europe were enemies.

A few months later Suleyman began his own war against the Christians. It could hardly have started more promisingly. The Ottomans already possessed most of what is now Greece, Bulgaria and Rumania. If you look at the map you will see that these two countries lie across the mouth of the great river Danube, which flows from the middle of Europe to the Black Sea. Suleyman's way into Europe lay up the Danube. Barring his way was the fortress of

The Selimye Mosque: The architect Sinan thought this was his greatest building

Belgrade, placed just where the Danube flowed through difficult mountains. In 1521 Suleyman captured Belgrade, the gateway to Hungary and Central Europe. Francis I of France was taken prisoner by Charles V. The French appealed to the Sultan to attack Charles. For the rest of Suleyman's reign the French were either his allies or friendly onlookers while he attacked the Emperor's lands. Charles was bitter about Francis's most un-Christian behaviour.

In 1526 Suleyman won the greatest of his victories against the Christians. At the Battle of Mohacs in Hungary the Turkish infantry, the Janissaries, (D5, 6) and his light armed cavalry the Sipahis were too strong for the heavy armed cavalry of the Hungarians. King Louis of Hungary was killed in the battle. This led to direct war between the Ottomans and the rulers of Austria. Suleyman attacked the Austrian capital of Vienna. (D7) He failed to take it; but Christian Europe had not been in such danger from a Muslim army since Arab forces marched into France eight hundred years before. For three weeks in 1529, the defenders of the Austrian capital looked out across the splendid and colourful tents of Suleyman's great army. The Ottomans were defeated as much by the terrible weather that dogged them from the moment they left Istanbul in May as by the efforts of the enemy. They arrived before the walls of Vienna too late to give themselves a reasonable chance of taking the city before winter. In the middle of October they were forced to begin the long march back to Istanbul or run the risk of being cut off from their base. (D7) In order to hold on to Hungary, Suleyman had to fight six more campaigns before he died.

Suleyman fought the Christians at sea as well as on land. In the Mediterranean he did this largely with the help of Barbarossa, leader of the Barbary pirates. For much of Suleyman's reign Turkish ships threatened Spanish trade and possessions in the western Mediterranean. The final battles in the struggle for control of the Mediterranean were fought just after Suleyman's death. In 1570 the Turks captured Cyprus in a large-scale land and sea operation. The Turks kept Cyprus; but they were never again a threat in the western Mediterranean.

In 1498 the Portuguese explorer, Vasco da Gama, sailed round the Cape of Good Hope, up the east coast of Africa and across to India. The rich trade of the Indian Ocean had been controlled for centuries by Muslim peoples. Since their victory over the Mamluks the Ottomans had had a fleet in the area. Suleyman sent a fleet to help the Muslims in north-west India; but it failed to drive the Portuguese from their base. The future on the seas lay with those powers who were already building ships more suited to the rougher conditions of the world's oceans. It was not the Turks but the Dutch and the English who eventually replaced the Portuguese in the Indian Ocean. (On European expansion eastwards: *Spices and Civilizations*)

Not all Suleyman's wars were fought against the Christians. The

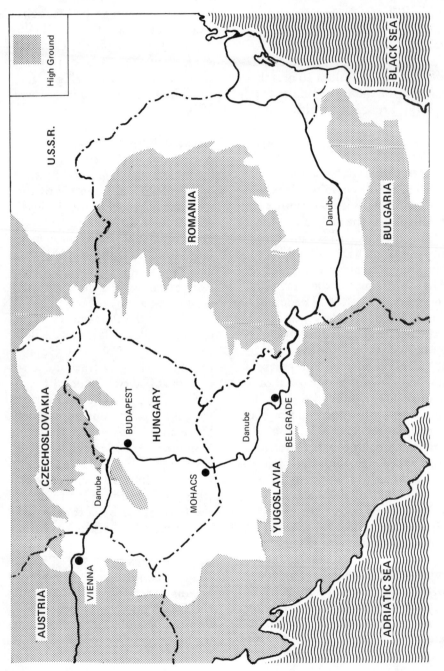

Suleyman's route to Vienna

The Battle of Mohacs

Muslim world, like the Christian world, was divided. In the Christian west there were Catholics and Protestants; in the Muslim lands there were *Sunnis,* like the Turks, and *Shi'ites* like the Persians. Rivalry between the Turks and Persians flared up again in 1533. Suleyman called off a war in Hungary to march against them. Later a second war broke out between the two great Muslim powers. It was in this year that the English traveller Anthony Jenkinson saw Suleyman's army passing through Aleppo. (D8) With the army went thousands of camels and mules to carry the tons of supplies needed. (D9) After these campaigns Ottoman control was firmly established in the valleys of the Tigris and Euphrates. Further east on the Persian plateau the land they won was lost again at the beginning of the next century.

Suleyman was already nearly sixty years old at the time of his second Persian campaign and his health was not always good. But he had little rest from war. Duty kept him campaigning to the last and he died in his tent whilst his army was besieging a Hungarian fortress. He had fought thirteen campaigns, most of them success-

Suleyman's army besieging Vienna

ful. He was buried in the great mosque named after him, the Suleymaniye. The Ottomans never had so powerful a Sultan again. The poet Baki wrote a lament for his master. Even the great Sultan, the lion of war, he writes, has to come to the inevitable end of all men:

That master-rider of the realm
    of bliss
For whose careering steed the
    field of the world was narrow
The infidels of Hungary bowed
    their heads to the temper of
    his blade,
The Frank [French] admired
    the grain of his sword.
He laid his face to the ground,
    graciously, like a fresh rose
    petal,
The treasurer of time put him
    in the coffer, like a jewel.

THE OTTOMAN ARMY AND OTTOMAN GOVERNMENT

The successes and achievements of Suleyman's reign owe much to the Sultan himself. But Suleyman had in his service many great men in many different fields. Above all he had a splendid army.

Suleyman's army was the greatest army of its time. European writers compared it with their armies and found it much better. It was larger, more obedient, and well-equipped. Where European armies lived off the land, causing great suffering to all the people of the countries in which they fought, many of the Ottoman soldiers lived in barracks

— years before such special quarters were built in Europe.

Suleyman's army consisted of four parts. First were the *Sipahis*. These were horsemen, armed with the lance, the sabre and the bow. They were paid by grants of land and they lived on their lands when they were not fighting. Second were the *Tatars*. These were the light horsemen from the Crimea and the steppe lands of the Ukraine. They raided far ahead of the main Ottoman armies, pinning the enemy down and bringing back news of his plans. Third was the artillery. The Ottoman guns were good; many were bought from Europe. Last and best known were the *Janissaries*. These were the slave infantry who formed the core of the Ottoman army. They were by origin Christians who had been converted to Islam. They were trained in the arts of war from an early age. They were skilled with their long guns and their long knives. Their charge was a terrifying thing to face. In defence they were dogged and difficult to beat. They were entirely loyal to the Sultan at this time, although later, when the Empire declined, this was not so.

All these people, Janissaries, ministers in the Government, Baki the poet, were slaves who were the property of the Sultan. They were recruited from his non-Muslim subjects. In the early days they were mostly prisoners of war. But later a more reliable method was found for recruiting the Sultan's servants. This was called the *devshirme* or levy of boys. (D10) The boys were sorted

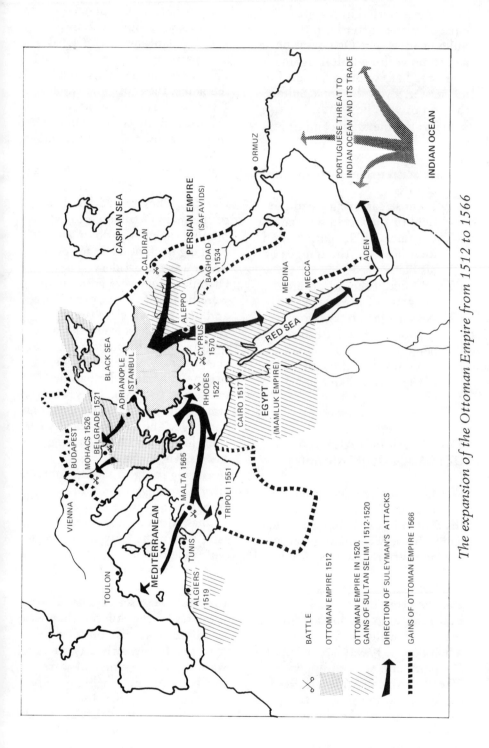

The expansion of the Ottoman Empire from 1512 to 1566

The personal sign of Suleyman which headed the texts of his orders

according to ability for different kinds of service. (D11) Those who were chosen for the most important posts remained in the Sultan's palace. Their training was long and difficult. They had to become skilled in many different fields. They passed through four 'schools', spending normally five to six years in each one. (D12) They began to learn Turkish and were instructed in the religion of Islam in Arabic. In the second school their study of languages continued; and regular physical exercises started. These included wrestling, shooting with a bow, tossing the pike, throwing the mace and handling other weapons. Before they passed on into the third school they were men, strong and fit for anything. Military training and learning a trade

'necessary for the service of the King's person' was an important part of their preparation in the third school. At this stage they also had to show that they were likely to remain true to their new religion. If they completed these first stages of their training they were registered for the fourth school. At this point their pay was raised and they dressed in silk and cloth of gold. From them the Sultan chose the leading officials of the household.

It is no wonder that the Ottomans were able to achieve great things in so many different fields when the Sultan's officials and servants received such a thorough training. Those who were unable to become imperial officials were sent off into the provinces under the care of Muslim

17

A janissary in full uniform

lords. There they led a life meant
to harden and toughen them.
Eventually they were returned by
their owners to Istanbul where the
best of them were enrolled as
young janissaries. (D11)

Foreign visitors to the Sultan's
court were impressed by the men
turned out by this system. One of
these visitors was Ghiselin de
Busbecq. He was a Fleming who
went to Istanbul in 1554 as the
ambassador of Ferdinand of
Austria. Busbecq stayed in Istanbul
until 1562 and during this time he
got to know Suleyman and his
people better than most
westerners. The colour and
splendour of Suleyman's court and

even more the discipline and order
of the great gathering impressed
him. (D13) He trembled to think
of the result if the Turks attacked
his own people.

The highest position that
anyone could rise to in the
Ottoman Empire was that of
Grand Vizier. He was the Sultan's
chief adviser. Mehemed the
Conqueror was the first Sultan to
appoint one of his 'slave' household as Vizier, recruited from the
Christian lands and trained in the
palace schools. From that time
all the Sultan's advisers were
chosen in this way.

By Suleyman's reign the Sultan
no longer attended the council of

The Grand Vizier rides with his attendants

chief ministers who met in a room of the palace called the divan chamber. The Grand Vizier took the Sultan's place at these meetings. One of Suleyman's Grand Viziers was Lufti Pasha. He was recruited in the devshirme. After training in the palace schools he held various offices including those of chief taster and chief gate warden. Next he had experience as a provincial official and then as governor of an important province. He went on several campaigns under both Selim I and Suleyman. He became Grand Vizier in 1529. Two years later he was dismissed. He was married to the Sultan's sister and in a moment of anger he was rude to his wife. This could have meant severe punishment, but he was more fortunate than many. He was allowed to retire and live in peace on his estate. He studied and wrote books. One of these was a little manual on the office and duties of a Grand Vizier. In this he passed on some hints and advice for the benefit of his successors.

The Grand Vizier must be a devout Muslim and set an example to others. He must never accept bribes and must make sure that all posts are filled according to merit and ability. He should try to keep down taxation and to control prices in the interests of the poor. (D14) In spite of his great power and responsibility he is the Sultan's servant and liable to sudden dismissal.

Lufti Pasha's dismissal underlined the importance of the Sultan in the Ottoman state. Suleyman's personal qualities help to explain the successes of his reign. What kind of man was he? Ambassadors from western countries have left several descriptions of him, mostly from the last ten years of his reign. A little earlier, however, an envoy from Ferdinand discovered that he could be roused to terrible anger by what he regarded as dishonesty and double-dealing. (D15) All describe Suleyman as an impressive figure, a man of great

Decorated tiles show the great craftsmanship of Muslim artists

dignity and regal bearing. By 1560 he had already achieved much and wanted only to be allowed to live in peace and keep what he had won. He would not hesitate to fight, however, in defence of his lands and his faith in spite of his age and his poor health. Almost all writers emphasize his sense of justice, a quality which earned him the title used by his own people – Suleyman the Lawgiver. (D16)

OTTOMAN ACHIEVEMENTS

The achievements of the Ottomans were already great by the death of Suleyman. They were the leading people in the Muslim world. They defeated in war all their rivals. At the height of their power under Suleyman they ruled an empire stretching from Algiers in the west to the Persian Gulf in the east; from the Crimea in the north to Aden in the south. They devised a system for raising and training soldiers and officials which worked well for over two hundred years. They were tolerant to non-Muslims in their empire although they made them pay heavier taxes. The mosques and other buildings in Istanbul and other towns and cities are a proof of their greatness as builders, craftsmen, and artists. Their empire lasted longer than most and did not finally disappear until after the First World War.

THE DECLINE OF THE OTTOMAN EMPIRE

The decline of the empire began after the reign of Suleyman. None of his successors had his great qualities. At first decline was slow. In 1683, for example, Ottoman armies were once again outside the gates of Vienna. It was not until 1699 that they were at last forced to surrender Hungary to the Austrians. By this time another reason for their decline was clear. Great changes in science and technology were taking place in western Europe. *(The Scientific Revolution* and *The Industrial Revolution)* The west was producing new weapons and inventing new military tactics. The Turks were lagging behind in all these ways. They suffered defeats at the hands of the Austrians in the late seventeenth century and the Austrians and Russians in the eighteenth century. In spite of attempts at reform in the nineteenth century the decline continued. At this time the non-Muslim peoples began to rise against the Sultan. Nationalism gained strength in Greece and Rumania, Serbia and Bulgaria. All these people had broken free from Istanbul before 1900. In the First World War the Arab subjects of the empire, though they were Muslims, seized the chance to break away from Turkish rule. Ottoman fortunes had turned full circle. Under a new leader, Kemal Ataturk, the Ottoman Empire and the Sultanate were ended. Turkey became a Republic in 1923. The new Turkey, with the exception of the old capital of Istanbul, lay in Asia Minor where the Ottoman State had first begun over six hundred years earlier.

DOCUMENT 1

SULTAN MEHEMED BEGINS THE SIEGE OF CONSTANTINOPLE
ZORZI DOLFIN — A fifteenth-century Greek chronicler

He [Mehemed] caused to be brought saltpetre and sulphur, with quantities of copper and he assembled German gunfounders paying them high wages. Wherever and whenever he wishes he has bombards (cannon) cast; as for the bombards not transportable because of their great size, he has them reduced to a number of pieces, so that it is possible to take them where he wants to go. . . .God, therefore, angered over the sins of the Christians rebellious to his law, sent against them Mehemed the most potent emperor of the Turks, a young man bold, ambitious and a mortal foe of the Christians. On 5th April 1453 he arrived to pitch his camp before Constantinople, with 300,000 soldiers; and round about the city he set his tents. Three days later, having occupied the walls on the landward side, Mehemed caused to be brought forward innumerable guns and instruments of war, with mantlets of interwoven material before the outer walls as a protection for the assailants. And with other smaller machines of war the Ottomans sought on all sides to ruin the walls of the city.

DOCUMENT 2

MEHEMED THE CONQUEROR PLANS WORLD CONQUEST
GIACOMO LANGUSTO — A Venetian visitor to Turkey

Every day he [Mehemed II] has Roman and other histories read him. . . . Diligently he seeks information on the position of Italy and how many kingdoms there are in Europe, of which he has a map showing the states and provinces. Nothing gives him greater satisfaction and pleasure than to study the state of the world and the science of war. A shrewd explorer of affairs, he burns with the desire to rule. . . .The Empire of the world, he says, must be one, one faith and one kingdom. To make this unity there is no place in the world more worthy than Constantinople.

DOCUMENT 3

THE BUILDING OF THE SULEYMANIYE MOSQUE   *EVLIYA CHELEBI — A seventeenth-century Turkish writer and traveller*

Suleyman having assembled all the thousands of perfect masters in architecture, building, stone-hewing and marble-cutting, three whole years were spent in laying the foundations. The workmen penetrated so far into the earth, that the sound of their pick-axes was heard by the bull that bears up the world at the bottom of the earth. In three more years the building reached the face of the earth; but in the ensuing year the building was suspended, and the workmen were employed in sawing and cutting various coloured stones for building above the foundations. In the following year the Mihrab [prayer niche] was fixed and the walls, which reached the vault of heaven, were completed. On those four solid foundations they placed its lofty dome. . . .On the side next to the Mihrab, and on that opposite to it, the dome is joined by two semi-domes. . . .Sinan opened windows on every side to give light to the mosque. . . .On the right and left of the Mihrab there are spirally twisted columns, which appear like the work of magic. . . .This mosque has four minarets, the galleries of which are ten in number, as a record that Sultan Suleyman was the tenth Sultan of the House of Osman.

DOCUMENT 4

VISITORS FROM THE WEST MARVEL AT THE BEAUTY OF THE SULEYMANIYE MOSQUE   *EVLIYA CHELEBI*

When it was finished the architect Sinan said to the Sultan: 'I have built for thee, O Emperor, a mosque which will remain on the face of the earth until the day of judgement.'

The humble writer of these lines once himself saw ten Frankish infidels skilful in geometry and architecture, who, when the doorkeeper had changed their shoes for slippers, and had introduced them into the mosque for the purpose of showing it to them, laid their fingers on their mouths, and each bit his finger for astonishment when they saw the minarets; but when they beheld the dome they tossed up their hats and cried Maria, Maria; and on observing the four arches which support the dome. . .they could not find terms to express their admiration, and the ten, each laying his finger on his mouth, remained a full hour looking with astonishment on these arches. Afterwards, on surveying the exterior, the court, and its four minarets, six gates, its columns, arches and cupolas, they again took off their hats and went round the mosque bareheaded, that being their manner of testifying their great amazement. One of them said that in the whole of Frangistan [western Europe] there was not a single edifice which could be compared to this.

DOCUMENT 5

THE JANISSARIES   *BARON WENCESLAS WRATISLAW – A Bohemian nobleman in Istanbul at the end of the sixteenth century*

The Janissaries are much regarded as being the Turkish Emperor's household troops. They are infantry and attend on the Sultan's person, to the number of twelve thousand; they wear long garments down to the instep, but of cloth not of silk. Instead of hats they wear a kind of sleeve, into the wider end of which they put their heads; these are different at each end, and one hangs down the neck as far as the back; whereas there is a tube of silver gilt set with pearls and the more ordinary precious stones, in front over the forehead. In this in wartime they place feathers.

DOCUMENT 6

THE JANISSARIES   *GHISELIN DE BUSBECQ – A Flemish nobleman and Austrian ambassador to Suleyman*

The Turks take the utmost care to keep their soldiers in good health and protected from the inclemency of the weather; hence, one sees the Turk better clothed than armed. He is particularly afraid of the cold, against which, even in the summer, he guards himself by wearing three garments, of which the innermost—call it shirt or what you will—is woven of coarse thread and provides much warmth. As a further protection against cold and rain tents are always carried, in which each man is given just enough space to lie down, so that one tent holds twenty-five or thirty Janissaries. The material for the garments to which I have referred is provided at the public expense. To prevent any disputes or suspicion of favour, it is distributed in the following manner. The soldiers are summoned by companies in the darkness to a place chosen for the purpose where are laid out ready as many pieces of cloth as there are soldiers in the company; they enter and take whatever chance offers them in the darkness, and they can only ascribe it to chance whether they get a good or bad piece of cloth.

DOCUMENT 7

THE OTTOMAN CAMPAIGN AGAINST VIENNA, 1529   *from THE OFFICIAL TURKISH JOURNAL*

May 1529
10	Departure from Istanbul
12-13	Driving rain, great cold
20	Adrianople [Edirne]

29   March in driving rain

June
5   Philippopolis [Plevdiv]
9   Rain
10-11   A halt; the waters of the Maritza river rise above the
           bridge; men and horses drowned; a great number of
           soldiers pass two days and two nights on the trees which
           they climbed to escape the flood.
20   Sofia
30   Nish

July
17   Belgrade
20   Eski Hisarlik; execution of a sipahi [cavalryman] accused
           of having let his horse graze in the fields under cultivation.
31   Camp near Vukovar; endless rain.

August
5   The army arrives at the banks of the Drava river, near
           Osijek.
7   The Grand Vizier remains near the walls of Osijek in order
           to fill the marshes with fascines [bundles of brushwood]
           for the passage of the army.
9   The marshes are filled with fascines.
10   A bridge thrown over the Drava.
15-16   A halt made; a storm; nine men killed by lightning. All
           the troops having crossed the Drava, the Sultan orders
           the bridge to be cut. The crossing had taken six days.
19   Mohacs. Zapolya admitted to audience with the Sultan
           [Zapolya was the Sultan's vassal in Hungary].
21   A halt; waiting for the arrival of the Danube flotilla with
           provisions and stores.

September
3   The Sultan encamps amid the vineyards of Buda.
8   Buda capitulates.
27   The Sultan arrives before Vienna; rain throughout the
           night.
30   Cold rain and wind.

October
2   Mehemed Beg of Semendria repels a sortie of the beseiged
           Christians.

5	The Begs of Semendria and Bosnia receive the order to mine the walls; the troops of Anatolia are at work filling the ditches with fascines.
9	Two mines fired off and new breaches made—a fruitless assault against the breaches in the walls; a stubborn conflict, above all on the sector of the Beg of Semendria.
12	Two new mines open large breaches in the walls; a council held of the Begs of Rumeli [the Balkan territories under Ottoman rule] in the tent of the Vizier. The cold and the lack of food becoming more and more pressing; the decision is taken to retreat; but preparations are made for one last assault.
14	Mines fired off and new breaches made—a vain assault. Orders given for the return to Istanbul.
15	[Some of] the guns taken aboard the Danube flotilla; the raiders bring a large number of prisoners to the camp.
16	Departure from Vienna.

DOCUMENT 8

THE OTTOMAN ARMY AS IT ENTERS ALEPPO ON ITS WAY TO FIGHT THE PERSIANS, 1553 *ANTHONY JENKINSON – An English traveller*

Immediately after them came the Great Turke himselfe, with great pompe and magnificence, using in his countenance and gesture a wonderfull majestie, having onely on each side of his person one page clothed with cloth of golde: he himselfe was mounted upon a goodly white horse, adorned with a robe of cloth of golde, embroidered most richly with the most pretious stones, and upon his head a goodly white tuck, containing in length by estimation fifteene yards, which was of silke and linen woven together, resembling something Callicut cloth, but is much more fine and rich, and in the toppe of his crowne a little pinnach of Ostrich feathers, and his horse most richly apparelled in all points correspondent to the same.

After marched the Great Basha, cheefe conductor of the whole army, clothed with a robe of crimson, and upon the same another short garment very rich, and about him fiftie Janizaries afoote, all clothed in crimson velvet, being armed as the Great Turkes own Janizaries.

So the whole army of the Grand Signior, containing as well those that went by the mountains, as also those that came to Aleppo in company with him, with horsemen and footemen, and the conductors of the camels and victuals, were the number of three hundred thousand.

The camels which carried munition and victuals for the saide army were in number two hundred thousand.

DOCUMENT 9

HOW THE OTTOMAN ARMY ORGANIZES ITS FOOD SUPPLIES
GHISELIN DE BUSBECQ

The Sultan, when he sets out on campaign, takes as many as forty
thousand camels with him, and almost as many baggage mules, most of
whom, if his destination is Persia, are loaded with cereals of every kind,
especially rice. The territories called Persia are much less fertile than our
country; and, further, it is the custom of the inhabitants, when their land
is invaded, to lay waste and burn everything, and so force the enemy to
retire through lack of food. The latter, therefore, are faced with serious
peril, unless they bring an abundance of food with them. They reserve
their supplies as far as possible for the return journey. . . .It is only then
that the Sultan's store of provisions is opened, and just enough food to
sustain life is weighed out each day to the Janissaries and the other
troops in attendance on him. The other soldiers are badly off, if they
have not provided food for their own use; most of them take a horse on
a leading rein loaded with the necessities of life. These include a small
piece of canvas to use as a tent, also some clothing and bedding and a
private store of provisions, consisting of a leather sack or two of the
finest flour, a small jar of butter and some spices and salt. They take a
few spoonfuls of flour and place them in water, adding a little butter,
and then flavour the mixture with salt and spices. This, when it is put on
the fire, boils and swells up so as to fill a large bowl. They eat of it once
or twice a day. They thus contrive to live on short rations for a month
or even longer if necessary. Some soldiers take with them a little sack
full of beef dried and reduced to a powder which is of great benefit as a
more solid form of nourishment.

DOCUMENT 10

THE 'DEVSHIRME' OR LEVY OF CHRISTIAN BOYS
BERNARDO NAVAGERO – A Venetian ambassador to Istanbul

An order is sent out with an officer of the Janissaries, who has also a
scribe with him.
   And the officer assigned to this task departs from Istanbul, bearing
with him new garments equal in number to the recruits whom it is
intended to select for the Janissaries, and he goes to the farthest confines
of the areas allocated to him in the order. . . .Arrived there he summons

before him the eldest official of the district. This official calls together forthwith their sons. . . .The officer, with the assistance of the scribe, chooses then from each household the one who seems to him in age and character most fitted for that service—preference being given to recruits within the range of twelve to fifteen years.

They dress all the boys in a garb of long clothes reaching to the ground, with a tall cap bearing a plume, and they call them azam oglani or little Janissaries. . .and when they have gathered the number of recruits mentioned in the order they go straight to Istanbul. The Sultan orders the boys to be paraded before him. If a recruit seems suitable and makes a good impression, the Sultan causes him to be assigned to the Palace.

DOCUMENT 11

SELECTION AND TRAINING OF A JANISSARY   *BARON WENCESLAS WRATISLAW*

Surgeons are on the spot, [at the time of the devshirme] who judge of the mental capacity of each individual child from his personal appearance, and determine for what future occupation he is likely to be fit. The most promising are selected for the service of the Turkish Emperor, the next class for that of the pashas and other Turkish officials; the remainder, who appear of less intellectual promise, are sold into Anatolia or Asia, to anyone who chooses to purchase them. They are kept till the appointed time—i.e., until they are eighteen or, at latest, twenty years old; are brought up in want, poverty, cold and heat, and are altogether treated little better than dogs: only whoever takes a boy is obliged to bring him back again to the Sultan's court. When about twenty years old, all embrowned with sun and heat, and accustomed to all kinds of labour, they are brought to Constantinople. There the most active are enrolled as young Janissaries and assigned to veteran Janissaries to learn to shoot, to use the sabre, to fling darts, to leap over trenches, and to scale walls. They are bound to obey every order given to them by the elder Janissaries, to prepare their food, cleave wood, and perform every necessary service as long as peace lasts. When they march with the elder soldiers to war they are still obliged to wait upon them, to pitch their tents, and to look after the camels and mules which carry the provisions and necessaries. On occasion of a battle or skirmish they march in the van, and endeavour to surpass each other in valour and steadfastness; nor are any of these taken into the ranks of the veteran janissaries till they have borne themselves like heroes.

DOCUMENT 12

THE BOYS CHOSEN FOR THE SULTAN'S SERVICE BEGIN THEIR TRAINING IN THE PALACE SCHOOLS _ROBERT WITHERS – A seventeenth-century English visitor to Turkey_

It now remayneth that I say somewhat of those Youths which are kept in better fashion in the Serraglio, for the King and Countreyes Service, brought up in Learning, in the knowledge of the Lawes, and in Military Exercises, that they may be able to perform those things, which belong to the Government of the whole Empire.

They have Roomes, which the Turkes call Oda's, but we may more properly call them Schooles; of which there are foure. Now into the first they all come, when they are but children, where the Primarie Precept they learne is Silence; then their personall Positures, betokening singular reverence to the King; which is, that they hold downe their heads and looke downwards, holding their hands before them joyned across.

Then they are set to learne to write and reade, and to practise the Turkish Tongue; and are taught their prayers in the Arabian tongue. Now, for the most part, they all stay about five or six yeeres in this Schoole, and such as are dull and hard of apprehension stay longer.

DOCUMENT 13

AT THE COURT OF SULTAN SULEYMAN, 1555 _GHISELIN DE BUSBECQ_

The Sultan was seated on a rather low sofa, not more than a foot from the ground and spread with many costly coverlets and cushions embroidered with exquisite work. . . .

In all that great assembly no single man owed his dignity to anything but his personal merits and bravery; no one is distinguished from the rest by his birth. . . .Those who hold the highest posts under the Sultan are very often the sons of shepherds and herdsmen, and the less they owe to their forefathers and to the accident of birth, the greater is the pride which they feel. They do not consider that good qualities can be conferred by birth or handed down by inheritance, but regard them partly as the gift of heaven and partly as the product of good training and constant toil and zeal. . . .This is why the Turks succeed in all that they attempt and are a dominating race and daily extend the bound of their rule. Our method is different; there is no room for merit, but everything depends on birth. . . .

Now come with me and cast your eye over this immense crowd of turbaned heads, wrapped in countless folds of the whitest silk, and bright raiment of every kind and hue, and everywhere the brilliance of gold, silver, purple, silk and satin. . . .No mere words could give an adequate idea of the novelty of the sight. A more beautiful spectacle was never presented to my gaze. . . .

What struck me as particularly praiseworthy in that great multitude was the silence and good discipline. . . .The most remarkable body of men was several thousand Janissaries, who stood in a long line apart from the rest and so motionless that, as they were at some distance from me, I was for a while doubtful whether they were living men or statues, until, being advised to follow the usual custom of saluting them, I saw them all bow their heads in answer to my salutation.

DOCUMENT 14

THE DUTIES OF THE OFFICE OF GRAND VIZIER   *LUFTI PASHA – Grand Vizier to Sultan Suleyman, 1539-41*

First and foremost, he who is Grand Vizier must have no private purpose or spite. Everything he does should be for God and in God and for the sake of God, for above this there is no higher rank to which he could attain. He should tell the Sultan the truth, without fear or concealment . . . .The secrets which the Grand Vizier shares with the Sultan must be withheld not only from outsiders, but even from the other viziers. . . .

The Grand Vizier should speak to the Sovereign, without hesitation, of what is necessary in the affairs of both religion and the State, and should not be held back by fear of dismissal. It is better to be dismissed and respected among men than to render dishonest service.

DOCUMENT 15

SULEYMAN IS FURIOUS TO LEARN THAT FERDINAND OF AUSTRIA HAS ATTACKED HUNGARY   *HIERONYMUS LASKI – An envoy of Ferdinand I of Austria to Suleyman*

I came therefore to the Sultan at about noon and, having kissed his hand, I greeted him in the name of my Royal Master [Ferdinand of Austria] . . . . I declared that my master the King had ever shown to His Majesty the Sultan, by what right and justice the realm of Hungary should belong to himself. . . .Hereupon the Sultan said: 'Do you recall the answer which I gave you?' I replied that I remembered it. The Sultan said: 'Have you told these things to your King?' I replied that I had told him. 'If then you have told him that I said the Kingdom is mine, wherefore has he sent an army into my Kingdom? And you, why have you come hither? Where now is your honesty? Your King strove to deceive me well, he sought a truce over so long a time that the summer would be gone and meanwhile he was arming himself to attack Buda. . . .' The Sultan said: 'Behold it is winter now, but summer will come again.' And thereafter he was in a great anger and spoke much, mingling in his speech violent reproaches. And now the Pashas bade me not to utter one word more, but to go out. I left with the Sultan still shouting in his fury. The Pashas remained with the Sultan for three hours and then it was decreed that the the Sultan should go to Adrianople and that he should declare and proclaim war.

DOCUMENT 16

DESCRIPTIONS OF SULEYMAN   *GHISELIN DE BUSBECQ*

You will probably wish me to describe the impression which Suleyman made upon me. He is beginning to feel the weight of years, but his dignity and his general physical appearance are worthy of the ruler of so vast an empire. He has always been frugal and temperate, and was so even in his youth, when he might have erred without incurring blame in the eyes of the Turks. Even in his earlier years he did not indulge in wine or in those unnatural vices to which the Turks are often addicted. . . .He is a strict guardian of his religion and its ceremonies, being not less desirous of upholding his faith than of extending his dominions. For his age—he has almost reached his sixtieth year—he enjoys quite good health, though his bad complexion may be due to some hidden malady; and indeed it is generally believed that he has an incurable ulcer or gangrene on his leg. This defect of complexion he remedies by painting his face with a coating of red powder, when he wishes departing ambassadors to take with them a strong impression of his good health; for he fancies that it contributes to inspire greater fear in foreign potentates if they think that he is well and strong.

ANTONIO BARBARIGO – Venetian ambassador to Suleyman, 1558

He is a just prince, mild and most religious in the observance of the law. Although when a young man he was aggressive and given to war, it is now clear that, being old, he desires peace with all princes and will never make war on anyone unless compelled thereto either by those against whom he enters into conflict or by the mistaken persuasion of his ministers. He knows that he is lord of many lands and wishes to enjoy in peace the dominions that he holds.

GHISELIN DE BUSBECQ

Those who saw Suleyman's face in this hour of triumph [on the return of his fleet after their victory over the Spaniards at Jerba, North Africa in 1560] declare that they could not detect any traces of unusual elation. Certainly I myself, when I saw him two days later, remarked that his expression was unaltered. His countenance was marked by the same sternness and sadness, so that you would almost have thought that the victory was no concern of his and that nothing new or unexpected had happened. So steeled was the old man's heart to accept whatever fortune might decree, so unflinching his mind, that he seemed to accept all the applause without emotion.

ANDREA DANDOLO – Venetian ambassador to Suleyman, 1562

He is held by all men to be very wise and just, but ruthless beyond measure against those who attempt or, in his judgement, may attempt something either against his empire or against his own person. He makes strict observance of religion and gives great regard to the law—a prince now turned towards the quiet life and intent on nothing more than to leave behind him an empire undisturbed, peaceful and secure.

ACKNOWLEDGMENTS

B.T. Batsford Ltd page 20; Sonia Halliday pages 13, 14, 17; The Mansell Collection pages 8, 18; Paul Popper Ltd pages 7, 9, 10.

5941

Greenhaven World History Program

History Makers
Alexander
Constantine
Leonardo Da Vinci
Columbus
Luther, Erasmus and Loyola
Napoleon
Bolivar
Adam Smith, Malthus and Marx
Darwin
Bismarck
Henry Ford
Roosevelt
Stalin
Mao Tse-Tung
Gandhi
Nyerere and Nkrumah

Great Civilizations
The Ancient Near East
Ancient Greece
Pax Romana
The Middle Ages
Spices and Civilization
Chingis Khan and the Mongol Empire
Akbar and the Mughal Empire
Traditional China
Ancient America
Traditional Africa
Asoka and Indian Civilization
Muhammad and the Arab Empire
Ibn Sina and the Muslim World
Suleyman and the Ottoman Empire

Great Revolutions
The Neolithic Revolution
The Agricultural Revolution
The Scientific Revolution
The Industrial Revolution
The Communications Revolution
The American Revolution
The French Revolution
The Mexican Revolution
The Russian Revolution
The Chinese Revolution

Enduring Issues
Cities
Population
Health and Wealth
A World Economy
Law
Religion
Language
Education
The Family

Political and Social Movements
The Slave Trade
The Enlightenment
Imperialism
Nationalism
The British Raj and Indian Nationalism
The Growth of the State
The Suez Canal
The American Frontier
Japan's Modernization
Hitler's Reich
The Two World Wars
The Atom Bomb
The Cold War
The Wealth of Japan
Hollywood

Greenhaven World History Progran